50 HULA WORKOUTS

Let's start Hooping!

Hannah Hoop

For questions, feedback and suggestions:
info@pisionary.com

Original edition
Hannah Hoop
ISBN Print: 9798740738208
1st Edition 2021
© 2021 pisionary Verlag (pisionary publishing)

All rights reserved, in particular the right of reproduction and distribution as well as translation. No part of this work may be reproduced in any form (by photocopy, microfilm or any other process) or stored, processed, duplicated or distributed using electronic systems without the written permission of the publisher.

Content

1   Hula Hoop: The Basics

11   Hula Hoop: Full Body Workouts

63   Hula Hoop: Special Workouts

115   Explanations of the exercises

Hula Hoop:
The Basics

Have you hooped today?

We all remember Hula Hoop from our childhood. We remember the carefree time back when we eagerly tried to let the colorful hoop circle around our hips in the schoolyard or at the playground. Even if we only succeeded for a few seconds, Hula Hoop immediately put a warm smile on our faces. But the colorful hoops are much more than just a toy for children. Hula Hoop also has a lot to offer for adults! In recent years, a Hula hoop trend has emerged. Whether just as a fun activity for in-between or to define the body and lose excess weight, more and more people let their hula hoops circle around their hips.

In this book you will learn how hooping affects your body, what to look for when buying hoops and how to hoop your way to your dream body. This book offers you 50 different Hula Hoop workouts. Whether you're just getting started with hooping or you've already mastered it: Here you will find exercises for every fitness level. Every single exercise is explained in a comprehensible way with numerous illustrations. So what are you waiting for? Grab your hoop and start hooping!

Hula Hoop - a success story

Throughout history there have been many cultures that used a hoop to exercise coordination and dexterity. As early as 400 years before Christ, the ancient Greeks recommended a so called hoop walk to their sick people to stimulate blood circulation. Indians and the Inuit also used hoops to playfully learn hunting techniques.

The hoop trend of the modern age did not begin until 1958, when the Californian toy manufacturer Wham-O was the first to start mass-producing hoops made of plastic. Prior to that, hoops were made of wood. Wham-O decided to name the plastic hoops Hula Hoop and then began to market them on a large scale. Hula is a native Hawaiian dance. In less than four months, 25 million Hula Hoops were sold in the U.S. and the colorful hoop became a staple in every child's room. In the same year, the Hula Hoop also reached the UK and other European countries.

More than just a hoop

Hula Hoop is more than just a simple game-fun for in-between. With the help of the hoop, the entire body can be trained effectively. With the right exercises, all muscle groups can be trained, defined and strengthened. Both long endurance and explosive strength workouts are possible. The hoop is ready for training immediately and, unlike other equipment, does not need to be set up for a long time. In addition, Hula Hoops can easily be stored and do not need much space.

In a nutshell, hooping can be done anywhere without much preparation and is therefore ideally suited for mothers and working people with little time. At the same time, the risk of injury while hooping is extremely low. Compared to most other sports, tendons and joints are not overly strained.

Hooping never gets boring and is addictive in a positive way. Because as you'll see, you can do a lot more with your hoop than just letting it circle around your hips.

Effects on body and soul

Hooping gets your whole body moving. The midsection consisting of the torso, abdomen, back and waist as well as the muscles of the buttocks and legs are particularly involved. In these parts of the body, the connective tissue and the skin are tightened and cellulite is reduced. Hardly any other exercise can define, tighten and model the problem area of the tummy, legs and bum so effectively.
Hooping boosts the metabolism and burns lots of calories. Depending on the intensity of the workout, up to 400 calories can be burned per hour. You will notice this on the scale very soon if you train regularly.

The whole body composition changes: while on the one hand excess weight drops, on the other hand muscles are built up. With a little discipline and the right training, anyone can hoop their way to their personal dream body.

Hooping makes you relaxed and loose. Muscle tensions and stiffness are dissolved You will become more limber and supple. Neck and back pain will soon be forgotten.

Hooping stabilizes the trunk and back muscles, which leads to a straighter posture. Unlike other fitness exercises, hopping does not train individual muscles in isolation, but rather the entire body is worked evenly. The pelvic floor is also strengthened through regular training, which is especially important for women after childbirth.

But not only our body benefits. Mind and soul are also positively influenced. Hooping stimulates the circulation. Tiredness and lack of energy disappear after just a few minutes. Happiness hormones flush the body and you feel great. Hooping is perfect to reduce stress and to get a clear head again. Through the movement, fear and worries often vanish in an instant.
Conclusion: Hula Hoop training is a true multi-talent. With hardly any other tool you can do something for your fitness and health so easily and have fun at the same time.

Choosing the right hoop

When you look for a suitable Hula Hoop in a store or on the Internet, you are literally overwhelmed by the choices. There are hoops in all possible sizes, shapes and colors. Everyone has different preferences with regard to the hoop. At the end of the day, the choice of hoop remains an individual matter. Nevertheless, there are some rules that always apply in principle and will help you in your choice.

Diameter

Regarding the diameter of the tire, the rule of thumb is that the hoop placed on the ground should go to your belly button or slightly above.

Hoop thickness

For beginners, a hoop thickness of about 2.5 cm is recommended. This way the hoop is heavy enough and stays better on your hips, which makes it easier to get started. Admittedly it sounds contradictory, but a heavy hoop is easier to hold up than a light hoop. Also make sure your hoop is sturdy enough and doesn't deform too easily. Especially beginners find hooping with sturdy hoops much easier. It is worthwhile to buy quality in order to avoid unnecessary trouble.

Tip: If you do not have much space at home or you are traveling a lot, make sure your hoop can be disassembled again after it has been put together. This is the case with most hoops. This way you can store the hoop in a space-saving way.

Hula Hoop types

There are a number of special Hula Hoop types, which are briefly presented below. Be sure to take enough time to find the right hoop. Above all, make sure the hoop feels comfortable to YOU.

- **Wavy hoop:** These hoops increase blood flow to the connective tissue.
- **Steel-core hoops:** These hoops are a little heavier, but they are extra stable. They do not bend as easily as plastic hoops.

- **Hoops with foam cover:** They are especially suitable for pressure-sensitive skin. They reduce the risk of bruises.
- **Hoops with extra weight:** these make the workout more strenuous, as the muscles have to work harder.
- **Hoops with pimples:** These are also known as massage hoops. The pimples will massage the connective tissue even more than ordinary hoops.
- **Electric Smart Hula Hoops:** These are equipped with electronics and record workout duration and calories burned. There are usually extra apps for these hoops that can be downloaded on your smartphone.

Children's hoops: Children's hoops are not suitable for adults. So if you've ever tried to hoop with a kid's hoop and it went all to hell, don't be surprised. They are too light and too small in diameter for adults.

Tip: If you buy your hoop in the store, you can immediately test several models and see how the hoops feel to you. In addition, individual consulting is possible this way.

Instruction - How to hoop

In the beginning, it's perfectly normal to not be able to control the hoop properly yet and for it to fall to the floor frequently. Do not let this discourage you. As with everything in life, practice makes perfect. Before you start:

- Make sure you have enough space around you.
- Wear tight-fitting clothes so that the hoop is not slowed down.
- Tie up long hair.
- Put on your sports shoes or work out barefoot.

The basic movement

Stable stance
Place your feet slightly wider than hip-width apart. Your feet can be at the same level or offset. Some people find it easier if their left or right foot is a little further forward. Find out what feels most comfortable to you and what gives you the best balance. If you prefer to hoop with one foot forward, you should occasionally put the other foot forward as well to give your muscles a balanced workout. Keep your knees loose and do not fully extend them.

The starting position
Now get into your hoop and hold it loosely with both hands. The hoop should be at about waist or belly button level and in contact with your lower back. Keep the hoop parallel to the ground.

The Swing

Give your Hula Hoop a strong swing with both hands to the right or left while releasing the hoop. As a beginner, you often may find one side easier than the other. This is perfectly normal. Later you can practice the other direction as well. With the proper swing, the hoop will circle around your waist 4-6 times by itself, without you having to move your hips. Try to feel how the hoop moves around your body.

The hip movement

When you have mastered the swing, you should try to keep the hula hoop up. As you do this, you need to move your hips. There are three different techniques to keep the Hula Hoop up and spinning.

The first technique is to move your hips from side to side. In doing this, you shift your weight from one leg to the other and back again. In the second technique, you move your hips forward and backward. In the last technique, you combine the first two techniques. Therefore, you circle your whole hip. It is always important to feel the Hula Hoop on your body and to use your hip movement to give the hoop momentum. Beginners often make the mistake of moving their hips uncontrollably and too fast, not following the rhythm of the Hula Hoop. If you move your hips at the right time, the hoop will maintain its speed and not fall down. Tighten your abdomen at all times. Your knees should always be slightly bent and your back straight.

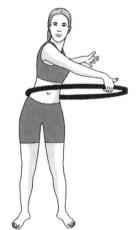

Tip: Your hip movements should not be too large. Make rather small and controlled movements to keep the hoop up.

The arms

You can bend your arms slightly or take them loosely upwards. You can hold your arms in all sorts of positions while hooping, such as folding your arms in front of your chest or making circular movements with your arms to work your shoulder muscles at the same time. Just make sure you don't pull your shoulders up, but keep them loose and relaxed.

Tip: If you notice that your hoop is gradually sliding down, try to squat down a little bit and bring the hoop back up by moving faster

Be patient

After a few days you will have internalized the basic movement and will be able to do it without thinking too much. Be patient with yourself! Practice makes perfect. Don't forget to practice the other direction as well.

For your understanding

With proper technique, the hoop touches your body in two places: once in the front, above the pelvic bone, and once in the back, above the gluteal bone. At these points of contact, you must give the hoop a swing by performing one of the three techniques. So the secret here is perfect timing

Bruises

As a beginner, you should get your skin used to the Hula Hoop at first to prevent bruises. Your first workouts with the hoop should therefore only be 3-5 minutes long. With time you can extend your workout and eventually your skin will get used to the hoop so you can hoop as long as you want. If you still get a few bruises, you may have very sensitive skin or a hoop that is too hard. But don't worry! The marks will soon disappear and with time, any skin gets used to hooping

Stick with it

You'll get the best results in terms of fat burning and muscle building if you exercise regularly. But also make sure you have enough rest periods. During these rest periods your body regenerates and builds new muscle cells. Too much muscle soreness can be a sign that you should take a break for a day or two. Then you will be able to start the training again and will be back stronger than before.

Tip: You should hoop both ways during each workout. For example, on the first cycle you hoop to the right and on the second to the left. In that way, all muscles will be worked evenly. Especially as a beginner you have a stronger direction. This is completely normal. With time you will master the other direction as well.

Stretching and cool down

Start each workout with a warm up and end each workout with a short cool down program. Stretch your body and bring your heart rate back down with slow movements.

The benefits of stretching are plentiful:
- Prevention of injury and improved circulation.
- More elastic tendons and muscles and better posture
- Release of tension and stiffness and better flexibility

Through regular workouts you will notice that you are developing more and more endurance and strength. In the mirror, you'll see your skin tighten and your muscles become more defined. Use your reflection in the mirror as an incentive to keep going.

Stretching exercises to warm up

About the Hula Hoop Workouts

In the following you will find 50 different hula hoop workouts that will help you target specific muscle groups. Please remember to start with workouts that are appropriate for your fitness level. That means a beginner should not start with a professional workout right away. Take it slow and soon you will be fit enough to do the advanced and professional workouts. The number of repetitions and exercise rounds are only guidelines that you can deviate from depending on your mood and your condition on the day. For example, instead of 40 seconds, you can hoop a full minute. Nevertheless, it is recommended that you adhere to the minimum guidelines for maximum training success. The exercises should be performed in the right order. It is recommended to alternate the hooping direction between the runs.

I wish you lots of fun and great success with your hooping journey. I will keep my fingers crossed that you will reach your goals. So get your hoop and let's go hooping!

Hula Hoop: Full Body Workouts

- For Beginners   13 - 32
- For Advanced Hoopers   33 - 52
- For Pros   53 - 62

Hula Hoop: Full Body Workouts 1 for Beginners

Estimated training duration: 12 min.

	Exercises	Repetitions/Time	Rest after exercise in sec.	Page
1	Hooping	40 sec.	20	/
2	Supported Squat	15 reps	20	126
3	Arms 3	40 sec.	20	117
4	Hula four-footer	30 sec.	20	131
5	Hooping	40 sec.	20	/
6	Supported lunges	8 reps	20	125

Two rounds with 20 seconds rest between exercises

1 Hooping | 40 sec.

2 Supported Squat | 15 reps

3 Arms 3 | 40 sec.

4 Hula four-footer | 30 sec.

5 Hooping | 40 sec.

6 Supported lunges | 8 reps

Hula Hoop: Full Body Workouts 2 for Beginners

Estimated training duration: 15 min.

	Exercises	Repetitions/ Time	Rest after exercise in sec.	Page
1	Hooping	40 sec.	20	/
2	Hooping jack	30 sec.	20	140
3	Arms 1	40 sec.	20	117
4	Pelvic lift	15 reps	20	124
5	Hooping in wide stance	40 sec.	20	118
6	Touch the hoop	30 sec.	20	129
7	Hooping	40 sec.	20	/
8	Rolling hoop	10 reps	20	133

Two rounds with 20 seconds rest between exercises

1 Hooping | 40 sec.

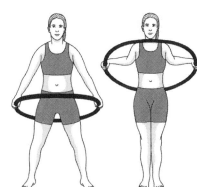
2 Hooping jack | 30 sec.

3 Arms 1 | 40 sec.

4 Pelvic lift | 15 reps

5 Hooping in wide stance | 40 sec.

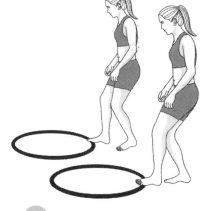
6 Touch the hoop | 30 sec.

7 Hooping | 40 sec.

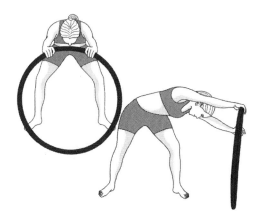
8 Rolling hoop | 10 reps

| 16

Hula Hoop: Full Body Workouts 3 for Beginners

Estimated training duration: 12 min.

	Exercises	Repetitions/ Time	Rest after exercise in sec.	Page
1	Hooping	40 sec.	20	/
2	Supported back kick	15 reps	20	125
3	Hooping tiptoes	40 sec.	20	119
4	Triceps press	15 reps	20	136
5	Arms 2	40 sec.	20	117
6	Wood Chopper	15 reps	20	132

Two rounds with 20 seconds rest between exercises

1 Hooping | 40 sec.

3 Hooping tiptoes | 40 sec.

5 Arms 2 | 40 sec.

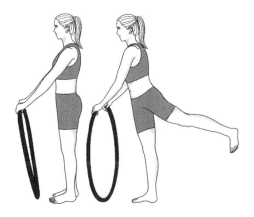

2 Supported back kick | 15 reps

4 Triceps press | 15 reps

6 Wood Chopper | 15 reps

Hula Hoop: Full Body Workouts 4 for Beginners

Estimated training duration: 12 min.

	Exercises	Repetitions/ Time	Rest after exercise in sec.	Page
1	Hooping	40 sec.	20	/
2	Supported Sumo Squat	15 reps	20	126
3	Hooping shifted	40 sec.	20	119
4	Shoulder press	15 reps	20	138
5	Hooping shifted	40 sec.	20	119
6	Kayaking	20 sec.	20	133

Two rounds with 20 seconds rest between exercises

1 Hooping | 40 sec.

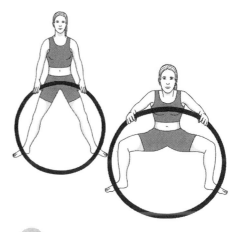

2 Supported Sumo Squat | 15 reps

3 Hooping shifted | 40 sec.

4 Shoulder press | 15 reps

5 Hooping shifted | 40 sec.

6 Kayaking | 20 sec.

Hula Hoop: Full Body Workouts 5 for Beginners

Estimated training duration: 12 min.

	Exercises	Repetitions/Time	Rest after exercise in sec.	Page
1	Hooping	40 sec.	20	/
2	Alternating jumps	15 reps	20	129
3	Hooping circling arms	20 sec.	0	120
4	Hooping	30 sec.	20	/
5	Back Pull	15 reps	20	135
6	Arms 3	40 sec.	20	117
7	Hoop Steering Wheel	30 sec.	20	138

◯ An empty circle means no rest after the exercise.

Two rounds with 20 seconds rest between exercises

1 Hooping | 40 sec.

2 Alternating jumps | 15 reps

3 Hooping circling arms | 20 sec.

4 Fast hooping | 30 sec.

5 Back Pull | 15 reps

6 Arms 3 | 40 sec.

7 Hoop Steering Wheel | 30 sec.

Hula Hoop: Full Body Workouts 6 for Beginners

Estimated training duration: 15 min.

	Exercises	Repetitions/Time	Rest after exercise in sec.	Page
1	Hooping	40 sec.	20	/
2	Hoop Mornings	15 reps	20	127
3	Hooping outside step	40 sec.	20	119
4	Hoop lift from prone position	10 reps	20	135
5	Hooping shifted	40 sec.	20	119
6	Basic Side Plank	20 sec.	30	130
7	Hooping	40 sec.	20	/
8	Knee push-up	10 reps	20	137

Two rounds with 20 seconds rest between exercises

1 Hooping | 40 sec.　　**2** Hoop Mornings | 15 reps　　**3** Hooping outside step | 40 sec.

4 Hoop lift from prone position | 10 reps　　**5** Hooping shifted | 40 sec.　　**6** Basic Side Plank | 20 sec.

7 Hooping | 40 sec.　　**8** Knee push-up | 10 reps

Hula Hoop: Full Body Workouts 7 for Beginners

Estimated training duration: 15 min.

	Exercises	Repetitions/Time	Rest after exercise in sec.	Page
1	Hooping	40 sec.	20	/
2	Lateral leg raises	15 reps	20	139
3	Hooping tiptoes	40 sec.	20	119
4	Front raises	15 reps	20	138
5	Arms 4	20 sec.	0	118
6	Fast hooping	30 sec.	20	/
7	Single leg pelvic lift	8 reps	20	125
8	Arms 5	40 sec.	20	118
9	Hoop Crunches	10 reps	30	131

Two rounds with 20 seconds rest between exercises

1 Hooping | 40 sec. **2** Lateral leg raises | 15 reps **3** Hooping tiptoes | 40 sec.

4 Front raises | 15 reps **5** Arms 4 | 20 sec. **6** Fast hooping | 30 sec.

7 Single leg pelvic lift | 8 reps **8** Arms 5 | 40 sec. **9** Hoop Crunches | 10 reps

Hula Hoop: Full Body Workouts 8 for Beginners

Estimated training duration: 20 min.

	Exercises	Repetitions/Time	Rest after exercise in sec.	Page
1	Hooping	40 sec.	20	/
2	Supported lunges	12 reps	20	125
3	Arms 1	40 sec.	20	117
4	Sailing in the wind	20 sec.	20	133
5	Hooping Walk	40 sec.	20	120
6	Shoulder press	15 reps	20	138
7	Hooping shifted	40 sek.	20	119
8	Diver	12 reps	20	136
9	Arms 3	40 sec.	20	117

Two rounds with 20 seconds rest between exercises

1. Hooping | 40 sec.
2. Supported lunges | 12 reps
3. Arms 1 | 40 sec.
4. Sailing in the wind | 20 sec.
5. Hooping Walk | 40 sec.
6. Shoulder press | 15 reps
7. Hooping shifted | 40 sec.
8. Diver | 12 reps
9. Arms 3 | 40 sec.

Hula Hoop: Full Body Workouts for Beginners

Estimated training duration: 20 min.

	Exercises	Repetitions/Time	Rest after exercise in sec.	Page
1	Hooping	40 sec.	20	/
2	Hoop Kick	12 reps	20	127
3	Hooping forward step	40 sec.	20	121
4	Triceps press	15 reps	20	136
5	Hooping outside step	40 sec.	20	119
6	Hooping in wide stance	40 sec.	0	118
7	Falling Hoop	30 sec.	20	139
8	Hula four-footer	30 sec.	20	131
9	Hooping shifted	40 sec.	20	119
10	Hoop lift from prone position	12 reps	20	135

Two rounds with 20 seconds rest between exercises

1 Hooping | 40 sec.
2 Hoop Kick | 12 reps
3 Hooping forward step | 40 sec.

4 Triceps press | 15 reps
5 Hooping outside step | 40 sec.
6 Hooping in wide stance | 40 sec.

7 Falling Hoop | 30 sec.
8 Hula four-footer | 30 sec.
9 Hooping shifted | 40 sec.
10 Hoop lift from prone position | 12 reps

Hula Hoop: Full Body Workouts 10 for Beginners

Estimated training duration: 20 min.

	Exercises	Repetitions/Time	Rest after exercise in sec.	Page
1	Hooping	40 sec.	0	/
2	Hooping jack	30 sec.	20	140
3	Arms 1	40 sec.	20	117
4	Kayaking	30 sec.	20	133
5	Arms 4	40 sec.	20	118
6	Hoop Mornings	15 reps	20	127
7	Hooping Walk	40 sec.	20	120
8	Knee push-up	12 reps	20	137
9	Hooping	40 sec.	20	/
10	Wall sit	30 sec.	20	130

○ An empty circle means no rest after the exercise.

31 | Hula Hoop: Full Body Workouts for Beginners

Two rounds with 20 seconds rest between exercises

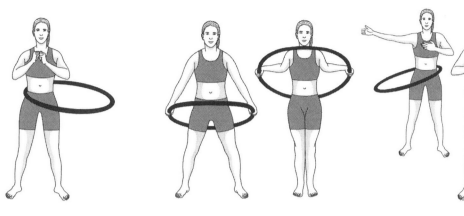

1 Hooping | 40 sec.   **2** Hooping jack | 30 sec.   **3** Arms 1 | 40 sec.

 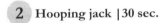 

4 Kayaking | 30 sec.   **5** Arms 4 | 40 sec.   **6** Hoop Mornings | 15 reps

7 Hooping Walk | 40 sec.   **8** Knee push-up | 12 reps   **9** Hooping | 40 sec.   **10** Wall sit | 30 sec.

Hula Hoop: Full Body Workouts 1 for Advanced Hoopers

Estimated training duration: 15 min.

	Exercises	Repetitions/Time	Rest after exercise in sec.	Page
1	Hooping	50 sec.	20	/
2	Hoop Squats	15 reps	20	126
3	Arms 2	50 sec.	20	117
4	Push-up	12 reps	20	137
5	Hooping 360°	4 reps	20	122
6	Hoop lift from prone position	15 reps	20	135
7	Fast hooping	50 sec.	20	/

Two rounds with 20 seconds rest between exercises

1 Hooping | 50 sec.

2 Hoop Squats | 15 reps

3 Arms 2 | 50 sec.

4 Push-up | 12 reps

5 Hooping 360° | 4 reps

6 Hoop lift from prone position | 15 reps

7 Fast hooping | 50 sec.

12 Hula Hoop: Full Body Workouts 2 for Advanced Hoopers

Estimated training duration: 15 min.

	Exercises	Repetitions/Time	Rest after exercise in sec.	Page
1	Hooping	50 sec.	20	/
2	Squat with hoop lift	15 reps	20	141
3	Hooping circling arms	50 sec.	20	120
4	Banana Hoop	12 reps	20	130
5	Hooping shifted	50 sec.	0	119
6	Fast hooping	30 sec.	20	/
7	One-arm triceps press	12 reps	0	136
8	Diver	12 reps	20	136

Two rounds with 20 seconds rest between exercises

1 Hooping | 50 sec.

2 Squat with hoop lift | 15 reps

3 Hooping circling arms | 50 sec.

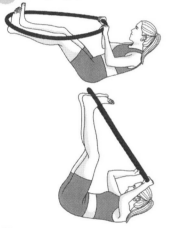

4 Banana Hoop | 12 reps

5 Hooping shifted | 50 sec.

6 Fast hooping | 30 sec.

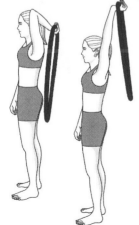

7 One-arm triceps press | 12 reps

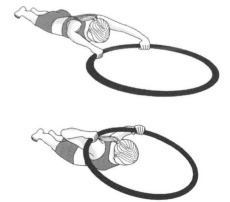

8 Diver | 12 reps

Hula Hoop: Full Body Workouts 3 for Advanced Hoopers

Estimated training duration: 18 min.

	Exercises	Repetitions/Time	Rest after exercise in sec.	Page
1	Fast hooping	50 sec.	20	/
2	Hoop Crunches	15 reps	20	131
3	Hooping in the squat	30 sec.	0	121
4	Hooping	50 sec.	20	/
5	Single leg pelvic lift	12 reps	20	125
6	Arms 5	30 sec.	0	118
7	Hooping forward step	30 sec.	20	121
8	Lat press	10 reps	20	135
9	Shoulder press	15 reps	20	138

Two rounds with 20 seconds rest between exercises

1 Fast hooping | 50 sec.

2 Hoop Crunches | 15 reps

3 Hooping in the squat | 30 sec.

4 Hooping | 50 sec.

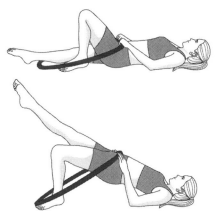
5 Single leg pelvic lift | 12 reps

6 Arms 5 | 30 sec.

7 Hooping forward step | 30 sec.

8 Lat press | 10 reps

9 Shoulder press | 15 reps

Hula Hoop: Full Body Workouts 4 for Advanced Hoopers

Estimated training duration: 20 min.

	Exercises	Repetitions/Time	Rest after exercise in sec.	Page
1	Hooping	50 sec.	20	/
2	Hoop Steering Wheel-Squat	40 sec.	20	140
3	Hoop Kick	15 reps	20	127
4	Hooping shifted	50 sec.	20	119
5	Hoop Plank	40 sec.	20	132
6	Arms 3	50 sec.	20	117
7	Triceps kick backs	12 reps	20	137
8	Arms 5	50 sec.	20	118
9	Hula four-footer	40 sec.	20	131

Two rounds with 20 seconds rest between exercises

1 Fast hooping | 50 sec.

2 Hoop Steering Wheel-Squat | 40 sec.

3 Hoop Kick | 15 reps

4 Hooping shifted | 50 sec.

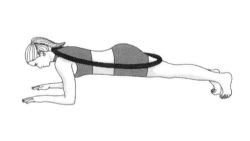

5 Hoop Plank | 40 sec.

6 Arms 3 | 50 sec.

7 Triceps kick backs | 12 reps

8 Arms 5 | 50 sec.

9 Hula four-footer | 40 sec.

Hula Hoop: Full Body Workouts 5 for Advanced Hoopers

Estimated training duration: 22 min.

	Exercises	Repetitions/Time	Rest after exercise in sec.	Page
1	Hooping	50 sec.	20	/
2	Back Pull	15 reps	20	135
3	Fast hooping	50 sec.	20	/
4	Front lift with back kick	12 reps	20	139
5	Hooping forward step	50 sec.	20	121
6	Diver	15 reps	20	136
7	Sailing in the wind	30 sec.	20	133
8	Hooping outside step	50 sec.	0	119
9	Hooping 360°	4 reps	20	122
10	Hoop Mornings	15 reps	20	127

○ An empty circle means no rest after the exercise.

Hula Hoop: Full Body Workouts 6 for Advanced Hoopers

Estimated training duration: 20 min.

	Exercises	Repetitions/Time	Rest after exercise in sec.	Page
1	Hoop lift	15 reps	20	127
2	Fast hooping	50 sec.	0	/
3	Hooping Walk	40 sec.	0	120
4	Hooping outside step	40 sec.	20	119
5	Side plank	30 sec.	20	134
6	Hula four-footer	30 sec.	20	131
7	One-arm triceps press	12 reps	20	136
8	Hooping	50 sec.	0	/
9	Squat hooping circling arms	30 sec.	20	121
10	Touch the hoop	40 sec.	20	129

Two rounds with 20 seconds rest between exercises

1 Hoop lift | 15 reps

2 Fast hooping | 50 sec.

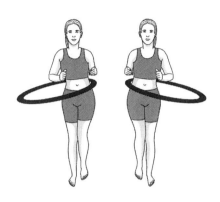

3 Hooping Walk | 40 sec.

4 Hooping outside step | 40 sec.

5 Side plank | 30 sec.

6 Hula four-footer | 30 sec.

7 One-arm tricpes press | 12 reps

8 Hooping | 50 sec.

9 Squat hooping circling arms | 30 sec.

10 Touch the hoop | 40 sec.

Hula Hoop: Full Body Workouts 7 for Advanced Hoopers

Estimated training duration: 20 min.

	Exercises	Repetitions/Time	Rest after exercise in sec.	Page
1	Hooping	50 sec.	0	/
2	Hooping back pull	30 sec.	0	120
3	Arms 3	30 sec.	0	117
4	Lunges	10 reps	20	124
5	Supported Sumo Squat	10 reps	20	126
6	Hoop Steering Wheel-Squat	30 sec.	20	140
7	Hoop lift from prone position	12 reps	20	135
8	Hooping Leg Raises	12 reps	40	132
9	Fast hooping	50 sec.	0	/
10	Hooping in wide stance	30 sec.	0	118

Hula Hoop: Full Body Workouts 8 for Advanced Hoopers

Estimated training duration: 22 min.

	Exercises	Repetitions/Time	Rest after exercise in sec.	Page
1	Hooping	50 sec.	0	/
2	Hooping circling arms	30 sec.	0	120
3	Arms 2	40 sec.	20	117
4	Lateral leg raises	10 reps	20	139
5	Hoop Squats	15 reps	0	126
6	Arms 4	50 sec.	0	118
7	Hooping tiptoes	30 sec.	20	119
8	Push-up	15 reps	20	137
9	Lat press	12 reps	20	135
10	Hoop Crunches	12 reps	20	131
11	Hula two-footer	25 sec.	20	131
12	Fast hooping	50 sec.	0	/
13	Low hooping	30 sec.	0	124

Two rounds with 20 seconds rest between exercises

1. Hooping | 50 sec.
2. Hooping circling arms | 30 sec.
3. Arms 2 | 30 sec.
4. Lateral leg raises | 10 reps
5. Hoop Squats | 15 reps
6. Arms 4 | 50 sec.
7. Hooping tiptoes | 30 sec.
8. Push-up | 15 reps
9. Lat press | 12 reps
10. Hoop Crunches | 12 reps
11. Hula two-footer | 25 sec.
12. Fast hooping | 50 sec.
13. Low hooping | 30 sec.

| 48

Hula Hoop: Full Body Workouts 9 for Advanced Hoopers

Estimated training duration: 22 min.

	Exercises	Repetitions/ Time	Rest after exercise in sec.	Page
1	Hooping jack	50 sec.	0	140
2	Hooping in the squat	30 sec.	0	120
3	Hooping shifted	50 sec.	20	119
4	Lunges	12 reps	20	124
5	Shoulder press	15 reps	20	138
6	Triceps kick backs	12 reps	20	137
7	Hooping with lateral leg raises	30 sec.	0	122
8	Hooping back kicks	30 sec.	0	122
9	Fast hooping	50 sec.	20	/
10	Back Pull	15 reps	20	135
11	Rolling hoop	30 sec.	20	133
12	Hoop Mornings	15 reps	20	127

Two rounds with 20 seconds rest between exercises

1. Hooping jack | 50 sec.
2. Hooping in the squat | 12 reps
3. Hooping shifted | 50 sec.
4. Lunges | 12 reps
5. Shoulder press | 15 reps
6. Triceps kick backs | 12 reps
7. Hooping with lateral leg raises | 30 sec.
8. Hooping back kicks | 30 sec.
9. Fast hooping | 50 sec.
10. Back Pull | 15 reps
11. Rolling hoop | 30 sec.
12. Hoop Mornings | 15 reps

| 50

Hula Hoop: Full Body Workouts 10 for Advanced Hoopers

Estimated training duration: 30 min.

	Exercises	Repetitions/Time	Rest after exercise in sec.	Page
1	Hooping	50 sec.	0	/
2	Arms 1	30 sec.	0	117
3	Arms 4	30 sec.	0	118
4	Hooping forward step	30 sec.	0	121
5	Hooping outside step	30 sec.	20	119
6	Squat with hoop lift	15 reps	20	141
7	Alternating jumps	30 sec.	20	129
8	Front lift with back kick	40 sec.	20	139
9	One-arm triceps press	15 reps	20	136
10	Single leg pelvic lift	12 reps	20	125
11	Banana Hoop	12 reps	0	130
12	Hula two-footer	25 sec.	30	131

◯ An empty circle means no rest after the exercise.

Three rounds with 20 seconds rest between exercises

1. Hooping | 50 sec.
2. Arms 1 | 30 sec.
3. Arms 5 | 30 sec.
4. Hooping forward step | 30 sec.
5. Hooping outside step | 30 sec.
6. Squat with hoop lift | 15 reps
7. Alternating jumps | 30 sec.
8. Front lift with back kick | 40 sec.
9. One-arm tricpes press | 15 reps
10. Single leg pelvic lift | 12 reps
11. Banana Hoop | 12 reps
12. Hula two-footer | 25 sec.

Hula Hoop: Full Body Workouts 1 for Pros

Estimated training duration: 25 min.

	Exercises	Repetitions/Time	Rest after exercise in sec.	Page
1	Squat mit Shoulder press	15 reps	20	140
2	Fast hooping	60 sec.	20	/
3	Pelvic lift	20 reps	20	124
4	Hooping in a lunge	60 sec.	20	123
5	Hula four-footer	60 sec.	20	131
6	Low hooping	60 sec.	20	124
7	Kayaking	20 reps	20	133
8	Lat press	20 reps	20	135
9	Hooping back pull	60 sec.	20	120
10	Triceps kick backs	15 reps	20	137

Two rounds with 20 seconds rest between exercises

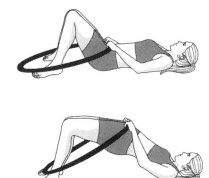

1. Squat mit Shoulder press | 15 reps
2. Fast hooping | 60 sec.
3. Pelvic lift | 20 reps

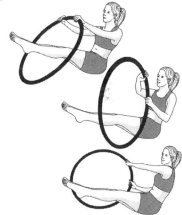

4. Hooping in a lunge | 60 sec.
5. Hula four-footer | 60 sec.
6. Low hooping | 60 sec.
7. Kayaking | 20 reps

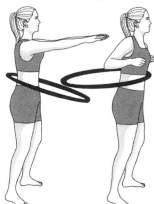

8. Lat press | 20 reps
9. Hooping back pull | 60 sec.
10. Triceps kick backs | 15 reps

Hula Hoop: Full Body Workouts 2 for Pros

Estimated training duration: 30 min.

	Exercises	Repetitions/ Time	Rest after exercise in sec.	Page
1	Eye of the needle	15 reps	20	134
2	Fast hooping	60 sec.	20	/
3	Falling Hoop	60 sec.	20	139
4	Wall sit	45 sec.	20	130
5	Hooping Walk	60 sec.	0	120
6	Hooping outside step	60 sec.	20	119
7	One-arm triceps press	20 reps	20	136
8	Banana Hoop	60 sec.	20	130
9	Sailing in the wind	30 sec.	20	133
10	Hooping	60 sec.	0	/
11	Hooping on one leg	30 sec.	20	123
12	Hoop Jumps	10 reps	20	128

Two rounds with 20 seconds rest between exercises

Hula Hoop: Full Body Workouts 3 for Pros

Estimated training duration: 25 min.

	Exercises	Repetitions/Time	Rest after exercise in sec.	Page
1	Hooping	60 sec.	0	/
2	Hooping back kicks	30 sec.	0	122
3	Hooping forward step	30 sec.	20	121
4	Squat hooping with circling arms	60 sec.	0	121
5	Hooping on one leg	30 sec.	0	123
6	Arms 2	30 sec.	20	117
7	Side lunge	10 reps	20	129
8	Front lift with back kick	20 reps	20	139
9	Diver	15 reps	20	136
10	Push-up	20 reps	20	137
11	Side plank	45 sec.	20	134
12	Hooping Leg Raises	15 reps	20	132

Two rounds with 20 seconds rest between exercises

1. Hooping | 60 sec.
2. Hooping back kicks | 30 sec.
3. Hooping forward step | 30 sec.
4. Squat hooping with circling arms | 15 reps
5. Hooping on one leg | 30 sec.
6. Arms 2 | 30 sec.
7. Side lunge | 10 reps
8. Front lift with back kick | 20 reps
9. Diver | 15 reps
10. Push-up | 20 reps
11. Side plank | 45 sec.
12. Hooping Leg Raises | 15 reps

Hula Hoop: Full Body Workouts 4 for Pros

Estimated training duration: 22 min.

	Exercises	Repetitions/ Time	Rest after exercise in sec.	Page
1	Hoop Burpees	10 reps	60	141
2	Hooping in a lunge	45 sec.	0	123
3	Hooping tiptoes	45 sec.	0	119
4	Fast hooping	60 sec.	20	/
5	Hoop Crunches	20 reps	20	131
6	Hula four-footer	60 sec.	20	131
7	Hoop lift from prone position	15 reps	20	135
8	Hooping shifted	60 sec.	0	119
9	Arms 1	45 sec.	0	117
10	Hooping with lateral leg raises	45 sec.	0	122

Two rounds with 20 seconds rest between exercises

1 Hoop Burpees | 10 reps   **2** Hooping in a lunge | 45 sec.   **3** Hooping tiptoes | 45 sec.

4 Fast hooping | 60 sec.   **5** Hoop Crunches | 20 reps   **6** Hula four-footer | 60 sec.

7 Hoop lift from prone position | 15 reps   **8** Hooping shifted | 60 sec.   **9** Arms 1 | 45 sec.   **10** Hooping with lateral leg raises | 15 reps

Hula Hoop: Full Body Workouts 5 for Pros

Estimated training duration: 45 min.

	Exercises	Repetitions/Time	Rest after exercise in sec.	Page
1	Hooping	60 sec.	0	/
2	Hoop In And Outs	30 sec.	20	128
3	Reversed overhead lunge	12 reps	40	128
4	Fast hooping	60 sec.	0	/
5	Hooping circling arms	30 sec.	0	120
6	Hooping on the knees	30 sec.	0	123
7	Hooping outside step	30 sec.	0	119
8	Hooping with lateral leg raises	30 sec.	0	122
10	Low hooping	60 sec.	30	124
10	Single leg pelvic lift	15 reps	20	125
11	Hula two-footer	45 sec.	20	131
12	Eye of the needle	10 reps	20	134
13	Lat press	15 reps	20	135
14	Knee push-up	20 reps	20	137

○ An empty circle means no rest after the exercise.

Three rounds with 20 seconds rest between exercises

1. Hooping | 60 sec.
2. Hoop In And Outs | 30 sec.
3. Reversed overhead lunge | 12 reps
4. Fast hooping | 60 sec.
5. Hooping circling arms | 30 sec.
6. Hooping on the knees | 30 sec.
7. Hooping outide step | 30 sec.
8. Hooping with lateral leg raises | 30 sec.
9. Low hooping | 60 sec.
10. Single leg pelvic lift | 15 reps
11. Hula two-footer | 45 sec.
12. Eye of the needle | 10 reps
13. Lat press | 15 reps
14. Knee push-up | 20 reps

| 62

Hula Hoop: Special Workouts

- Legs, Bums and Tums   65 - 74
- Burn Calories Special   75 - 82
- Arms Special   83 - 86
- Booty Special   87 - 90
- Abs Special   91 - 94
- Back Special   95 - 98
- Just Hooping   99 - 108
- Quick and fit   109 - 110
- Upright Posture Special   111 - 112
- Strong Core   113 - 114

Legs, Bums and Tums Hula Hoop Workout for Beginners I

Estimated training duration: 20 min.

	Exercises	Repetitions/Time	Rest after exercise in sec.	Page
1	Fast hooping	40 sec.	20	/
2	Supported Squat	15 reps	20	126
3	Hooping in wide stance	40 sec.	20	118
4	Pelvic lift	15 reps	20	124
5	Hooping back kicks	40 sec.	20	122
6	Hula four-footer	15 reps	20	131
7	Kayaking	30 sec.	20	133

Three rounds with 20 seconds rest between exercises

1 Fast hooping | 40 sec.

2 Supported Squat | 15 reps

3 Hooping in wide stance | 40 sec.

4 Pelvic lift | 15 Wdh.

5 Hooping back kicks | 40 sec.

6 Hula four-footer | 15 reps

7 Kayaking | 30 sec.

Legs, Bums and Tums Hula Hoop Workout for Beginners II

Estimated training duration: 18 min.

	Exercises	Repetitions/Time	Rest after exercise in sec.	Page
1	Hooping	40 sec.	20	/
2	Hoop Mornings	15 reps	20	127
3	Hooping tiptoes	30 sec.	0	119
4	Fast hooping	30 sec.	20	/
5	Supported Sumo Squat	15 reps	20	126
6	Hooping shifted	40 sec.	20	119
7	Hoop Plank	30 sec.	20	132
8	Basic Side Plank	20 sec.	20	130

Two rounds with 20 seconds rest between exercises

1 Hooping | 40 sec.

2 Hoop Mornings | 15 reps

3 Hooping tiptoes | 30 sec.

4 Fast hooping | 30 sec.

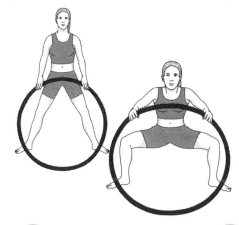

5 Supported Sumo Squat | 15 reps

6 Hooping shifted | 40 sec.

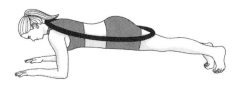

7 Hoop Plank | 30 sec.

8 Basic Side Plank | 20 sec.

28 Legs, Bums and Tums Hula Hoop Workout for Advanced Hoopers I

Estimated training duration: 20 min.

	Exercises	Repetitions/ Time	Rest after exercise in sec.	Page
1	Hooping Walk	50 sec.	0	120
2	Hooping in the squat	30 sec.	20	121
3	Reversed overhead lunge	12 reps	20	128
4	Lateral leg raises	12 reps	20	139
5	Supported back kick	12 reps	20	125
6	Fast hooping	50 sec.	0	/
7	Hooping outside step	30 sec.	20	119
8	Hoop Squats	10 reps	20	126
9	Hoop Crunches	15 reps	20	131
10	Sailing in the wind	30 sec.	20	133

Two rounds with 20 seconds rest between exercises

1. Hooping Walk | 50 sec.
2. Hooping in the squat | 30 sec.
3. Reversed overhead lunge | 12 reps
4. Lateral leg raises | 12 reps
5. Supported back kick | 12 reps
6. Fast hooping | 50 sec.
7. Hooping outside step | 30 sec.
8. Hoop Squats | 10 reps
9. Hoop Crunches | 15 reps
10. Sailing in the wind | 30 sec.

| 70

Legs, Bums and Tums Hula Hoop Workout for Advanced Hoopers II

Estimated training duration: 22 min.

	Exercises	Repetitions/Time	Rest after exercise in sec.	Page
1	Hooping shifted	50 sec.	0	119
2	Hooping in a lunge	30 sec.	20	123
3	Hoop lift	15 reps	20	127
4	Wall sit	40 sec.	20	130
5	Hoop Kick	12 reps	20	127
6	Fast hooping	50 sec.	0	/
7	Low hooping	30 sec.	0	124
8	Hooping 360°	4 reps	20	122
9	Pelvic lift	15 reps	20	124
10	Side plank	30 sec.	20	134
11	Hula two-footer	30 sec.	20	131

Two rounds with 20 seconds rest between exercises

1. Hooping shifted | 50 sec.
2. Hooping in a lunge | 50 sec.
3. Hoop lift | 15 reps
4. Wall sit | 40 sec.
5. Hoop Kick | 12 reps
6. Fast hooping | 50 sec.
7. Low hooping | 30 sec.
8. Hooping 360° | 4 reps
9. Pelvic lift | 15 reps
10. Side plank | 30 sec.
11. Hula two-footer | 30 sec.

| 72

Legs, Bums and Tums Hula Hoop Workout for Pros

Estimated training duration: 30 min.

	Exercises	Repetitions/Time	Rest after exercise in sec.	Page
1	Hooping	50 sec.	0	/
2	Hooping on one leg	20 sec.	20	123
3	Banana Hoop	15 reps	20	130
4	Kayaking	40 sec.	20	133
5	Side plank	30 sec.	20	134
6	Hooping in the squat	50 sec.	0	121
7	Hooping outside step	50 sec.	20	119
8	Reversed overhead lunge	12 reps	20	128
9	Side lunge	8 reps	30	129
10	Single leg pelvic lift	15 reps	30	125
11	Hula four-footer	50 sec.	20	131
12	Fast hooping	50 sec.	0	/
13	Hooping shifted	50 sec.	0	119
14	Hooping in wide stance	50 sec.	20	118
15	Hoop Mornings	15 reps	20	127

○ An empty circle means no rest after the exercise.

Two rounds with 20 seconds rest between exercises

1. Hooping | 50 sec.
2. Hooping on one leg | 20 sec.
3. Banana Hoop | 15 reps
4. Kayaking | 40 sec.
5. Side plank | 30 sec.
6. Hooping in the squat | 50 sec.
7. Hooping outside step | 50 sec.
8. Reversed overhead lunge | 12 reps
9. Side lunge | 8 reps
10. Single leg pelvic lift | 15 reps
11. Hula four-footer | 50 sec.
12. Fast hooping | 50 sec.
13. Hooping shifted | 50 sec.
14. Hooping in wide stance | 50 sec.
15. Hoop Mornings | 15 reps

| 74

Burn Calories Special I

Estimated training duration: 18 min.

	Exercises	Repetitions/Time	Rest after exercise in sec.	Page
1	Fast hooping	40 sec.	0	/
2	Touch the hoop	60 sec.	20	129
3	Arms 1	40 sec.	0	117
4	Hooping Walk	30 sec.	20	120
5	Hooping jack	40 sec.	20	140
6	Hoop Burpees	30 sec.	20	141

Three rounds with 20 seconds rest between exercises

① Fast hooping | 40 sec.

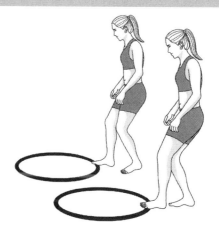

② Touch the hoop | 60 sec.

③ Arms 1 | 40 sec.

④ Hooping Walk | 30 sec.

⑤ Hooping jack | 40 sec.

⑥ Hoop Burpees | 30 sec.

Burn Calories Special II

Estimated training duration: 25 min.

	Exercises	Repetitions/Time	Rest after exercise in sec.	Page
1	Alternating jumps	40 sec.	0	129
2	Hooping jack	60 sec.	20	140
3	Fast hooping	40 sec.	0	/
4	Hooping Walk	30 sec.	0	120
5	Hooping circling arms	40 sec.	0	120
6	Squat with shoulder press	15 reps	20	140
7	Hoop Plank	30 sec.	0	132
8	Hooping tiptoes	60 sec.	40	119

77 | Burn Calories Special

Three rounds with 20 seconds rest between exercises

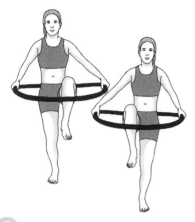

1 Alternating jumps | 40 sec.

2 Hooping jack | 60 sec.

3 Fast hooping | 40 sec.

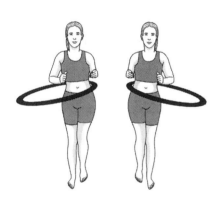

4 Hooping Walk | 30 sec.

5 Hooping circling arms | 40 sec.

6 Squat with shoulder press | 15 reps

7 Hoop Plank | 30 sec.

8 Hooping tiptoes | 60 sec.

Burn Calories Special III

Estimated training duration: 15 min.

	Exercises	Repetitions/ Time	Rest after exercise in sec.	Page
1	Fast hooping	40 sec.	20	/
2	Supported Sumo Squat	60 sec.	0	126
3	Supported back kick	40 sec.	20	125
4	Hooping jack	30 sec.	0	140
5	Arms 4	40 sec.	0	118
6	Hooping forward step	30 sec.	0	121
7	Hooping outside step	30 sec.	20	119
8	Hoop In And Outs	30 sec.	0	128
9	Touch the hoop	60 sec.	20	129

Two rounds with 20 seconds rest between exercises

1 Fast hooping | 40 sec. **2** Supported Sumo Squat | 60 sec. **3** Supported back kick | 40 sec.

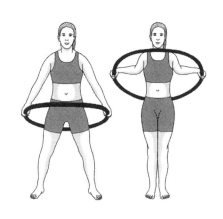  

4 Hooping jack | 30 sec. **5** Arms 4 | 40 sec. **6** Hooping forward step | 30 sec.

  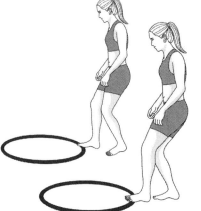

7 Hooping outside step | 30 sec. **8** Hoop In And Outs | 30 sec. **9** Touch the hoop | 60 sec.

Burn Calories Special IV

Estimated training duration: 18 min.

	Exercises	Repetitions/Time	Rest after exercise in sec.	Page
1	Fast hooping	40 sec.	20	/
2	Hoop Jumps	40 sec.	0	128
3	Hoop Kicks	40 sec.	20	127
4	Hooping jack	30 sec.	0	140
5	Low hooping	40 sec.	0	124
6	Hooping Walk	30 sec.	0	120
7	Hooping in the squat	40 sec.	20	121
8	Hoop Burpees	30 sec.	0	141
9	Hooping Leg Raises	30 sec.	20	132
10	Hooping in wide stance	40 sec.	0	118

Two rounds with 20 seconds rest between exercises

1 Fast hooping | 40 sec.   **2** Hoop Jumps | 40 sec.   **3** Hoop Kicks | 40 sec.

4 Hooping jack | 30 sec.   **7** Low hooping | 30 sec.   **6** Hooping Walk | 30 sec.   **5** Hooping in the squat | 40 sec.

8 Hoop Burpees | 30 sec.   **9** Hooping Leg Raises | 30 sec.   **10** Hooping in wide stance | 40 sec.

| 82

Arms Special 1
Hula Hoop Workout

Estimated training duration: 10 min.

	Exercises	Repetitions/Time	Rest after exercise in sec.	Page
1	Arms 5	40 sec.	0	118
2	One-arm triceps press	20 reps	20	136
3	Arms 1	40 sec.	0	117
4	Shoulder press	15 reps	20	138
5	Hooping circling arms	40 sec.	0	120
6	Knee push-up	15 reps	20	137

○ **An empty circle means no rest after the exercise.**

Two rounds with 20 seconds rest between exercises

1 Arms 5 | 40 sec.

2 One-arm triceps press | 20 reps

3 Arms 1 | 40 sec.

4 Shoulder press | 15 reps

5 Hooping circling arms | 40 sec.

6 Knee push-up | 15 reps

Arms Special 2
Hula Hoop Workout

Estimated training duration: 15 min.

	Exercises	Repetitions/Time	Rest after exercise in sec.	Page
1	Hooping	40 sec.	0	/
2	Triceps kick backs	15 reps	20	137
3	Hooping back pull	40 sec.	0	120
4	Falling Hoop	15 reps	20	139
5	Arms 4	40 sec.	0	118
6	Triceps press	15 reps	20	136
7	Hooping circling arms	40 sec.	0	120
8	Push-up	15 reps	20	137

Two rounds with 20 seconds rest between exercises

1 Hooping | 40 sec.

2 Triceps kick backs | 15 reps

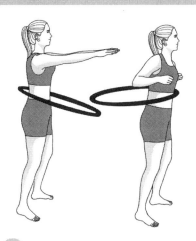

3 Hooping back pull | 40 sec.

4 Falling Hoop | 15 reps

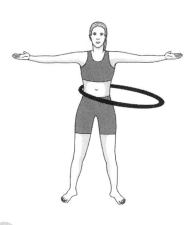

5 Arms 4 | 40 sec.

6 Triceps press | 15 reps

7 Hooping circling arms | 40 sec.

8 Push-up | 15 reps

| 86

Booty Special I
Hula Hoop Workout

Estimated training duration: 20 min.

	Exercises	Repetitions/Time	Rest after exercise in sec.	Page
1	Low hooping	40 sec.	0	124
2	Hooping in the squat	30 sec.	20	121
3	Supported back kick	20 reps	20	125
4	Lunges	15 reps	20	124
5	Hooping	60 sec.	20	/
6	Pelvic lift	20 reps	20	124
7	Hoop In And Outs	40 sec.	20	128
8	Hooping shifted	60 sec.	20	119

Two rounds with 20 seconds rest between exercises

1 Low hooping | 40 sec.
2 Hooping in the squat | 30 sec.
3 Supported back kick | 20 reps

4 Lunges | 15 reps
5 Hooping | 60 sec.
6 Pelvic lift | 20 reps

7 Hoop In And Outs | 40 sec.
8 Hooping shifted | 60 sec.

Booty Special II
Hula Hoop Workout

Estimated training duration: 20 min.

	Exercises	Repetitions/Time	Rest after exercise in sec.	Page
1	Hoop Squats	15 reps	20	126
2	Hooping in a lunge	50 sec.	20	123
3	Supported Sumo Squat	15 reps	20	126
4	Hooping back kicks	50 sec.	0	122
5	Hooping	50 sec.	20	/
6	Single leg pelvic lift	15 reps	20	125
7	Plank	60 sec.	20	132
8	Hoop Mornings	15 reps	20	127
9	Hooping in wide stance	50 sec.	20	118

Two rounds with 20 seconds rest between exercises

1 Hula Squat | 15 reps

2 Hooping in a lunge | 50 sec.

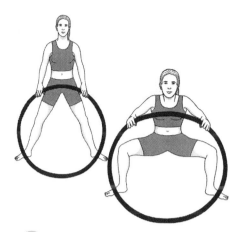

3 Supported Sumo Squat | 15 reps

4 Hooping back kicks | 50 sec.

5 Hooping | 50 sec.

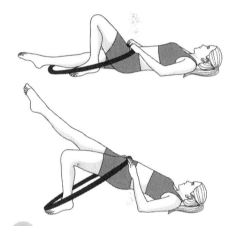

6 Single leg pelvic lift | 15 reps

7 Plank | 60 sec.

8 Hoop Mornings | 15 reps

9 Hooping in wide stance | 50 sec.

| 90

39 Abs Special I
Hula Hoop Workout

Estimated training duration: 20 min.

	Exercises	Repetitions/Time	Rest after exercise in sec.	Page
1	Hooping	60 sec.	20	/
2	Hooping on one leg	30 sec.	0	123
3	Hoop Crunches	20 reps	20	131
4	Hooping Leg Raises	15 reps	20	132
5	Hooping Walk	60 sec.	0	120
6	Low hooping	30 sec.	20	124
7	Hula four-footer	60 sec.	20	131
8	Basic Side Plank	30 sec.	20	130
9	Banana Hoop	15 reps	20	130

Two rounds with 20 seconds rest between exercises

  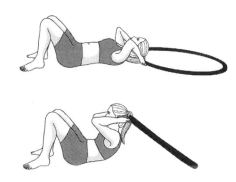

1. Hooping | 60 sec.
2. Hooping on one leg | 30 sec.
3. Hoop Crunches | 20 reps

  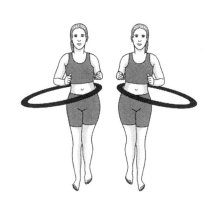 

4. Hooping Leg Raises | 15 reps
5. Hooping Walk | 60 sec.
6. Low hooping | 30 sec.

7. Hula four-footer | 60 sec.
8. Basic Side Plank | 30 sec.
9. Banana Hoop | 15 reps

40 Abs Special II
Hula Hoop Workout

Estimated training duration: 20 min.

	Exercises	Repetitions/ Time	Rest after exercise in sec.	Page
1	Side plank	45 sec.	20	134
2	Eye of the needle	15 reps	20	134
3	Hoop Plank	60 sec.	20	132
4	Kayaking	30 sec.	20	133
5	Hula two-footer	30 sec.	20	131
6	Hooping forward step	60 sec.	0	121
7	Low hooping	30 sec.	0	124
8	Hooping tiptoes	60 sec.	0	119
9	Hooping 360°	5 reps	20	122

○ An empty circle means no rest after the exercise.

Two rounds with 20 seconds rest between exercises

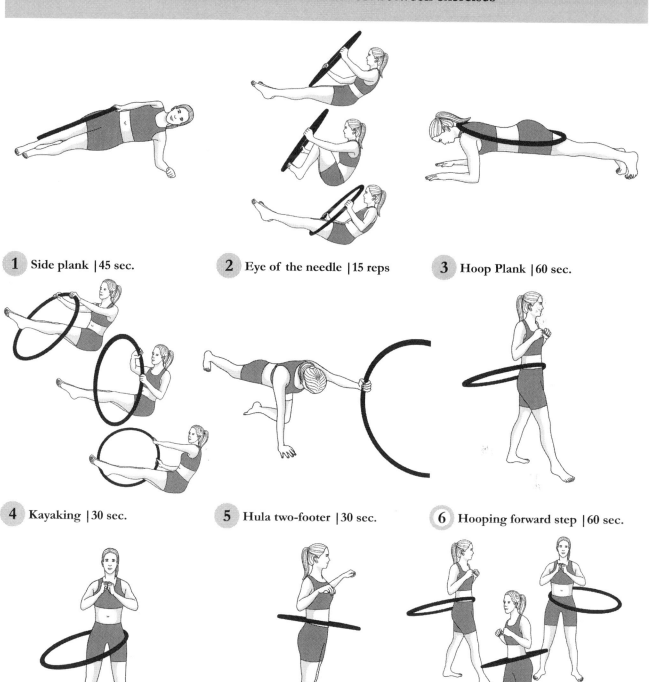

1. Side plank | 45 sec.
2. Eye of the needle | 15 reps
3. Hoop Plank | 60 sec.
4. Kayaking | 30 sec.
5. Hula two-footer | 30 sec.
6. Hooping forward step | 60 sec.
7. Low hooping | 30 sec.
8. Hooping tiptoes | 60 sec.
9. Hooping 360° | 5 reps

Back Special I
Hula Hoop Workout

Estimated training duration: 15 min.

	Exercises	Repetitions/Time	Rest after exercise in sec.	Page
1	Hoop lift	15 reps	20	127
2	Fast hooping	60 sec.	20	/
3	Back Pull	15 reps	20	135
4	Hooping back pull	60 sec.	20	120
5	Hoop Plank	50 sec.	20	132
6	Lat press	15 reps	20	135
7	Arms 2	60 sec.	20	117

Two rounds with 20 seconds rest between exercises

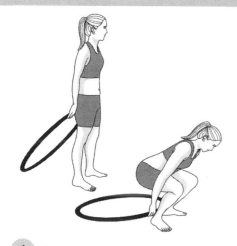

1 Hoop lift | 15 reps

2 Fast hooping | 60 sec.

3 Back Pull | 15 reps

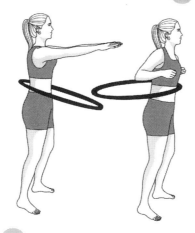

4 Hooping back pull | 60 sec.

5 Hoop Plank | 50 sec.

6 Lat press | 15 reps

7 Arms 2 | 60 sec.

| 96

Back Special II
Hula Hoop Workout

Estimated training duration: 15 min.

	Exercises	Repetitions/Time	Rest after exercise in sec.	Page
1	Hoop Mornings	20 reps	20	127
2	Hooping shifted	60 sec.	20	119
3	Low hooping	60 sec.	20	124
4	Diver	20 reps	20	136
5	Hooping back pull	60 sec.	0	120
6	Hooping circling arms	30 sec.	20	120
7	Hoop lift from prone position	15 reps	0	135
8	Fast hooping	60 sec.	0	/

Two rounds with 20 seconds rest between exercises

1 Hoop Mornings | 20 reps

2 Hooping shifted | 60 sec.

3 Low hooping | 60 sec.

4 Diver | 20 reps

5 Hooping back pull | 60 sec.

6 Hooping circling arms | 30 sec.

7 Hoop lift from prone position | 15 reps

8 Fast hooping | 60 sec.

| 98

Just Hooping I
Hula Hoop Workout

Estimated training duration: 5 min.

	Exercises	Repetitions/Time	Rest after exercise in sec.	Page
1	Hooping	45 sec.	0	/
2	Arms 1	45 sec.	0	117
3	Arms 2	45 sec.	0	117
4	Fast hooping	45 sec.	0	/
5	Hooping circling arms	45 sec.	0	120
6	Arms 3	45 sec.	0	117
7	Hooping in wide stance	30 sec.	0	118

One round

1. Hooping | 45 sec.
2. Arms 1 | 45 sec.
3. Arms 2 | 45 sec.

4. Fast hooping | 45 sec.
5. Hooping circling arms | 45 sec.

6. Arms 3 | 45 sec.
7. Hooping in wide stance | 30 sec.

Just Hooping II
Hula Hoop Workout

Estimated training duration: 7 min.

	Exercises	Repetitions/Time	Rest after exercise in sec.	Page
1	Hooping	60 sec.	0	/
2	Hooping shifted	30 sec.	0	119
3	Hooping back pull	60 sec.	0	120
4	Arms 3	30 sec.	0	117
5	Fast hooping	30 sec.	0	/
6	Hooping forward step	30 sec.	0	121
7	Arms 4	30 sec.	0	118
8	Low hooping	30 sec.	0	124
9	Hooping	60 sec.	0	/
10	Arms 5	30 sec.	0	118
11	Hooping in a lunge	30 sec.	0	123

One round

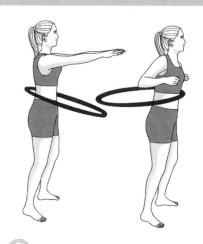

① Hooping | 60 sec.　　② Hooping shifted | 30 sec.　　③ Hooping back pull | 60 sec.

④ Arms 3 | 30 sec.　　⑤ Fast hooping | 30 sec.　　⑥ Hooping forward step | 30 sec.　　⑦ Arms 4 | 30 sec.

⑧ Low hooping | 30 sec.　　⑨ Hooping | 60 sec.　　⑩ Arms 5 | 30 sec.　　⑪ Hooping in a lunge | 30 sec.

45 Just Hooping III
Hula Hoop Workout

Estimated training duration: 10 min.

	Exercises	Repetitions/Time	Rest after exercise in sec.	Page
1	Fast hooping	60 sec.	0	/
2	Hooping circling arms	30 sec.	0	120
3	Hooping tiptoes	30 sec.	0	119
4	Arms 2	60 sec.	0	117
5	Arms 3	45 sec.	0	117
6	Hooping in the squat	45 sec.	0	121
7	Hooping	60 sec.	0	/
8	Hooping Walk	30 sec.	0	120
9	Hooping shifted	60 sec.	0	119
10	Low hooping	30 sec.	0	124
11	Hooping 360°	30 sec.	0	122
12	Hooping back kicks	30 sec.	0	122
13	Hooping with lateral leg raises	30 sec.	0	122
14	Hooping	60 sec.	0	/

○ An empty circle means no rest after the exercise.

One round

① Fast hooping | 60 sec. ② Hooping circling arms | 30 sec. ③ Hooping tiptoes | 30 sec. ④ Arms 2 | 60 sec. ⑤ Arms 3 | 45 sec.

⑥ Hooping in the squat | 45 sec. ⑦ Hooping | 60 sec. ⑧ Hooping Walk | 30 sec. ⑨ Hooping shifted | 60 sec. ⑩ Low hooping | 30 sec.

⑪ Hooping 360° | 30 sec. ⑫ Hooping back kicks | 60 sec. ⑬ Hooping with lateral leg raises | 30 sec. ⑭ Hooping | 60 sec.

Just Hooping IV
Hula Hoop Workout

Estimated training duration: 15 min.

	Exercises	Repetitions/Time	Rest after exercise in sec.	Page
1	Hooping	120 sec.	0	/
2	Hooping Walk	60 sec.	0	120
3	Hooping outside step	45 sec.	0	119
4	Low hooping	45 sec.	0	124
5	Hooping	60 sec.	0	/
6	Hooping back pull	60 sec.	0	120
7	Squat hooping circling arms	45 sec.	0	121
8	Hooping circling arms	45 sec.	60	120
9	Arms 2	45 sec.	0	117
10	Hooping on one leg	60 sec.	0	123
11	Hooping with lateral leg raises	60 sec.	0	122
12	Fast hooping	60 sec.	0	/
13	Arms 5	30 sec.	0	118
14	Hooping in a lunge	60 sec.	0	123
15	Hooping forward step	30 sec.	0	121
16	Hooping on the knees	30 sec.	0	123

One round

1. Hooping | 120 sec.
2. Hooping Walk | 60 sec.
3. Hooping outside step | 45 sec.
4. Low hooping | 45 sec.
5. Hooping | 60 sec.

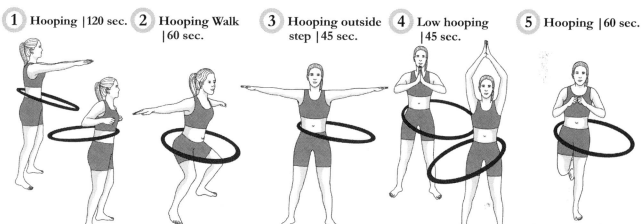

6. Hooping back pull | 60 sec.
7. Squat hooping circling arms | 45 sec.
8. Hooping circling arms | 45 sec.
9. Arms 2 | 45 sec.
10. Hooping on one leg | 60 sec.

11. Hooping lateral leg raises | 60 sec.
12. Fast hooping | 60 sec.
13. Arms 5 | 30 sec.
14. Hooping in a lunge | 60 sec.
15. Hooping forward step | 30 sec.
16. Hooping on knees | 30 sec.

| 106

47 Just Hooping! The Challenge for Pros

Complete as many rounds as possible. If the hoop falls down it's game over!

	Exercises	Repetitions/Time	Rest after exercise in sec.	Page
1	Hooping	20 sec.	0	/
2	Low hooping	20 sec.	0	124
3	Hooping	20 sec.	0	/
4	Hooping 360°	20 sec.	0	122
5	Hooping on one leg	20 sec.	0	123
6	Fast hooping	20 sec.	0	/
7	Low hooping	20 sec.	0	124
8	Hooping back pull	20 sec.	0	120
9	Hooping in the squat	20 sec.	0	121
10	Hooping	20 sec.	0	/
11	Hooping tiptoes	20 sec.	0	119
12	Hooping forward step	20 sec.	0	121
13	Hooping Walk	20 sec.	0	120
14	Hooping outside step	20 sec.	0	119
15	Hooping with lateral leg raises	20 sec.	0	122
16	Hooping back kicks	20 sec.	0	122
17	Hooping in wide stance	20 sec.	0	118

As many rounds as possible

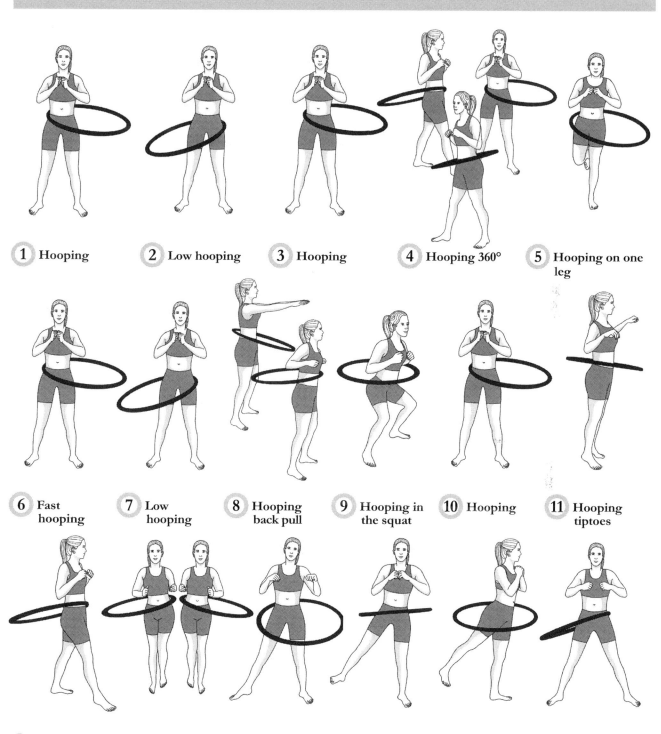

Quick and fit
Hula Hoop Workout

Estimated training duration: 10 min.

	Exercises	Repetitions/Time	Rest after exercise in sec.	Page
1	Hoop Burpees	50 sec.	0	141
2	Fast hooping	50 sec.	0	/
3	Low hooping	40 sec.	20	124
4	Alternating jumps	30 sec.	0	129
5	Squat hooping circling arms	50 sec.	0	121
6	Arms 2	40 sec.	20	117

Two rounds with 20 seconds rest between exercises

1 Hoop Burpees | 50 sec.

2 Fast hooping | 50 sec.

3 Low hooping | 40 sec.

4 Alternating jumps | 30 sec.

5 Squat hooping circling arms | 50 sec.

6 Arms 2 | 40 sec.

49 Upright Posture Special Hula Hoop Workout

Estimated training duration: 15 min.

	Exercises	Repetitions/Time	Rest after exercise in sec.	Page
1	Hooping back pull	50 sec.	0	120
2	Hooping back kicks	50 sec.	0	122
3	Arms 3	50 sec.	20	117
4	Hoop Mornings	15 reps	20	127
5	Front raises	20 reps	20	138
6	Reversed overhead lunge	8 reps	20	128
7	Wall sit	50 sec.	20	130

Two rounds with 20 seconds rest between exercises

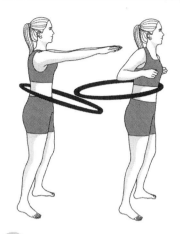

1 Hooping back pull | 50 sec.

2 Hooping back kicks | 50 sec.

3 Arms 3 | 50 sec.

4 Hoop Mornings | 15 reps

5 Front raises | 20 reps

6 Reversed overhead lunge | 8 reps

7 Wall sit | 50 sec.

| 112

Strong Core
Hula Hoop Workout

Estimated training duration: 20 min.

	Exercises	Repetitions/Time	Rest after exercise in sec.	Page
1	Pelvic lift	20 reps	20	124
2	Hoop Plank	30 sec.	20	132
3	Basic Side Plank	30 sec.	20	130
4	Supported Sumo Squat	20 reps	20	126
5	Hoop In And Outs	30 sec.	20	128
6	Sailing in the wind	30 sec.	20	133
7	Hooping in wide stance	30 sec.	0	118
8	Hooping shifted	30 sec.	0	119
9	Hooping on one leg	30 sec.	0	123
10	Hooping in the squat	30 sec.	0	121
11	Fast hooping	30 sec.	0	/
12	Hooping	30 sec.	20	/

○ An empty circle means no rest after the exercise.

113 | Strong Core

Two rounds with 20 seconds rest between exercises

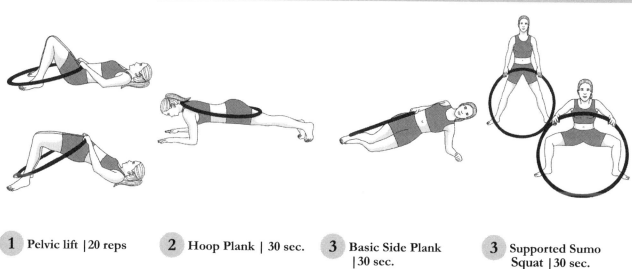

1 Pelvic lift | 20 reps **2** Hoop Plank | 30 sec. **3** Basic Side Plank | 30 sec. **3** Supported Sumo Squat | 30 sec.

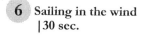

5 Hoop In And Outs | 30 sec. **6** Sailing in the wind | 30 sec. **7** Hooping in wide stance | 30 sec. **8** Hooping shifted | 30 sec.

9 Hooping on one leg | 30 sec. **10** Hooping in the squat | 30 sec. **11** Fast hooping | 30 sec. **12** Hooping | 30 sec.

| 114

Explanations of the exercises

- Hooping Exercises   117 - 123
- Lower Body Exercises   124 - 129
- Abdominal and core exercises 130 - 134
- Back exercises   135
- Arm-, chest and shoulder exercises 136 - 138
- Full Body Exercises   139 - 141

Hooping Exercises

Arms 1

As illustrated, while hooping, alternately extend one arm outward and place the palm of the other arm on the chest.

Arms 2

As in the illustration, while hooping, fold your arms in front of your chest and stretch them upward over head. Repeat this several times.

Arms 3

As in the illustration, while hooping, stretch your arms upward and hold them there.

117 | Hooping Exercises

Arms 4

Stretch your arms out to the sides while hooping. The palms of your hands point upward. Move your arms up and down a few inches so that you flutter like a butterfly.

Arms 5

Keep your arms in the position as shown in the picture while hooping.

Hooping in wide stance

Stand wider than usual while hooping.

Hooping outside step

While hooping, alternately step up with one foot to the side.

Hooping shifted

Hoop in shifted stance as shown in the illustration. Make sure that each leg is in front for about the same time.

Hooping tiptoes

Hoop on your tiptoes.

119 | Hooping Exercises

Hooping while circling your arms

Stretch your arms to the side while hooping and circle them forward or backward.

Hooping back pull

Extend your arms forward while hooping and pull them back as far as you can by contracting your shoulder blades.

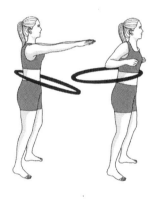

Hooping Walk

While hooping, alternately pull your legs together as if you were walking on the spot. You can also walk slowly around the room while hooping instead.

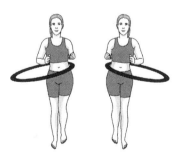

Hooping Exercises | 120

Hooping forward step

Take alternate short forward steps while hooping. Only briefly touch the floor in front of you with your front feet. Allow enough time between each step.

Hooping in the squat

While hooping squat down slightly. You can also either hold the squat permanently or do squats by bending up and down.

Squat hooping with circling arms

Squat down while you hoop. At the same time stretch your arms to the side and make circular movements with them.

Hooping 360°

Turn once in a circle while hooping. You can either turn with several small steps or with a sweeping turn on the ball of your foot.

Hooping with lateral leg raises

Alternately lift your legs briefly to the side while hooping.

Hooping with back kicks

Alternately lift your legs briefly backwards while hooping.

Hooping on one leg

Stand on one leg alternately while hooping. It is especially important to hold body tension.

Hooping on the knees

Try to slowly kneel down while hooping and then stand up again. This is a very difficult exercise.

Hooping in a lunge

Hoop in lunge as shown in the picture. The back leg is only on the front foot.

Low hooping

Let your hoop slow down. This lowers the Hula Hoop from the waist to the hips. Try to keep the hoop in this position by accelerating again.

Lower Body Exercises

Lunges

1. Get into starting position as shown in the picture.

2. Perform a forward lunge. Lower the back knee until it almost touches the floor. The front knee remains aligned over the midfoot and should not go further forward than the tips of the toes.

3. Then come back to the starting position and perform the lunge with both legs alternating.

Pelvic lift

1. Take starting position as shown in the picture.

2. Push the pelvis up as far as it will go by flexing the glute muscles. Hold this position for one second.

3. Lower the pelvis again and return to the starting position.

Lower Body Exercises | 124

Single leg pelvic lift

1. Take the starting position as shown in the illustration. One leg is bent, the other leg is stretched out on the floor.

2. Push the pelvis upward as far as possible by contracting the gluteus muscles. The extended leg is in the air. Hold this position for one second.

3. Lower the pelvis again and return to the starting position.

Note: the back of your head should always touch the floor.

Supported lunges

1. Take the starting position as shown in the illustration.

2. Perform a lunge forward. Use the hoop as a support. Lower the back knee until it almost touches the floor. The front knee will remain aligned over the midfoot and should go no further forward than the tips of the toes.
Then go back to the starting position. Repeat the exercise with the same leg until the number of repetitions is reached. Then start with the other leg.

Supported back kick

1. Take the starting position as shown in the picture.

2. Lift one leg as far back as it can go and tense the gluteus muscles. Bend the upper body slightly forward and use the Hula Hoop as a support. Make sure that the core remains tense and the back is not hyperextended.

3. Hold the leg in the final position for one second and then return to the starting position in a controlled manner.

Supported Squat

1. Take the starting position as shown in the illustration. Make sure your feet are shoulder-width apart. Point toes forward or slightly outward.

2. Bend your knees. Use the Hula Hoop as a support. The tips of your toes should not go over your knees.

3. Push yourself back up and return to the starting position.

Supported Sumo Squat

1. Take the starting position as shown in the illustration. The stance is wider than in a normal squat, which gives the inner thighs a stronger workout.

2. Bend your knees. Use the Hula Hoop as a support. The tips of your toes should not go over your knees.

3. Push yourself back up and return to the starting position.

Hoop Squats

1. Take the starting position as shown in the illustration. Make sure you are standing shoulder-width apart. Point toes forward or slightly outward.

2. Bend your knees. The tips of your toes should not go over your knees.

3. Press back up and return to the starting position.

Lower Body Exercises | 126

Hoop Mornings

1. Take the starting position as shown in the picture.

2. Push pelvis back and tilt torso forward. Keep the spine straight. Maintain tension in the core muscles and make sure the position of the knees does not change during the exercise.

3. Slowly straighten up and return to the starting position.

Hoop Kick

1. Hold the hoop with both hands parallel to the floor. Press the hoop lightly against your waist.

2. Alternately lift your legs and try to touch the Hula Hoop with your feet.

Hoop lift

1. Take the starting position as shown in the picture.

2. Bend your knees and keep your back straight.

3. Push yourself back up and return to the starting position.

Hoop Jumps

1. Step into your hoop.

2. Bend your knees slightly and jump to the right so that you land outside the hoop.

3. Step back into your hoop and now jump to the left.

Hoop In And Outs

1. Take the starting position as shown in the illustration.

2. Alternately step out of the hoop with one leg and do a side squat as shown in the illustration. Make sure your back is straight, your core is tight, and that your knees are always positioned over your mid-foot.

3. Put your leg back into the hoop again as you go up.

Reversed overhead lunge

1. Take starting position as shown in the illustration.

2. Do a lunge, alternating between putting one leg back while going down to the knees. Go down until the knee of the back leg almost touches the floor. The knee of the front leg should move as little as possible and should not go over the top of the toes.

Lower Body Exercises | 128

Side lunge

1. Take the starting position as shown in the illustration.

2. Alternately push one leg to the side while slowly kneeling with the other leg.

3. Press up and return to the starting position. Touch the hoop Touch the hoop with the toes of your feet alternately and as fast as you can.

Touch the hoop

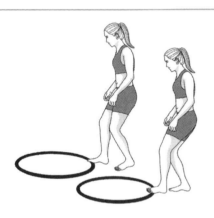

Tap the hoop with your front feet alternately and as fast as you can

Alternating jumps

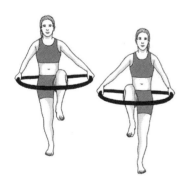

1. Get into your hoop. Keep the hoop parallel to the floor.

2. Jump alternately from one leg to the other. Raise your knees to your tummy as you do so.

Wall sit

1. Lean back against the wall and take a seated position. Your thighs should be parallel to the floor.

2. Hold the Hula Hoop in front of you as shown in the illustration.

3. Hold this position.

Abdominal and core exercises

Banana Hoop

1. Take the starting position as shown in the illustration. Only the buttocks touch the floor. The feet press lightly against the hoop and the hands pull the hoop slightly towards the head.

2. Roll backwards, pulling the hoop slightly towards you so that it almost touches your forehead. Keep your legs bent the same way at all times.

Basic Side Plank

1. Take the position as shown in the illustration: Both knees are bent on the floor. The elbow of the supporting arm is positioned directly under the shoulder. The forearm points straight forward.

2. Place the Hula Hoop on the hip bone and hold it firmly. Make sure your pelvis is pushed forwards and your torso is not sagging downwards. Knees, hips and shoulders must be in line. Maintain tension in this position.

Hula two-footer

1. Take the position as shown in the illustration. Be careful not to form a hunched back and not to hyperextend the head.

2. Hold this position.

Hula four-footer

1. Take the posture as shown in the illustration: Hands should be placed directly under the shoulder. The knees should remain under the hips.

2. Go up on your toes and keep your knees a few inches above the Hula Hoop. Make sure your knees never touch the Hoop.

3. Hold this position. While doing this, be careful not to go into a hunchback and not to hyperextend your head backwards.

Hoop Crunches

1. Take the starting position as shown in the illustration.

2. Slowly straighten up while keeping your Hula Hoop at the back of your head.

3. Slowly return to the starting position in a controlled manner.

Hoop Plank

1. Take the starting position as shown in the illustration. Elbows are placed under the shoulders. Thighs are in line with the pelvis and torso.

2. Keep your core muscles tight so that your spine maintains its normal curvature. Be careful not to hyperextend your back and do not to drop your abdomen.

Hold this position for the instructed amount of time.

Wood Chopper

1. Take the starting position as shown in the illustration.

2. Rotate torso left and right.

Hooping Leg Raises

1. Take the starting position as shown in the illustration. Only the buttocks and hands are on the floor. The legs should not touch the floor.

2. Raise your legs.

3. Return to the starting position. During the exercise your feet should never touch the floor.

Kayaking

1. Take the starting position as shown in the illustration. Only the buttocks touch the ground. The legs are extended.

2. Roll the Hula Hoop with your arms to the left and right so that the Hula Hoop is next to you. Make sure your legs move as little as possible and never touch the floor.

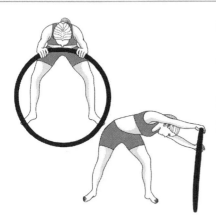

Rolling hoop

1. Take the starting position as shown in the illustration.

2. Roll the hoop in a semicircle to the left and right. Make sure your back is straight and you do not hyperextend your head.

Sailing in the wind

1. Take the starting position as shown in the illustration. Clamp the hoop between your feet and thighs. Only your forearms and buttocks are on the ground.

2. Turn your legs to the left and right.

133 | Abdominal and core exercises

Eye of the needle

1. Take starting position as shown in the illustration. Only the buttocks touch the floor.

2. Put your legs through the hoop.

3. Get your legs out of the hoop again and return to the starting position.

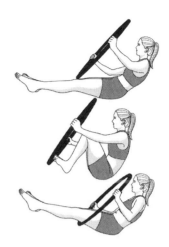

Side plank

1. Take the position as shown in the illustration. Only the feet and forearm touch the floor. The elbow of the supporting arm is placed directly under the shoulder. The forearm points straight forward.

2. Place the Hula Hoop on the hip bone and hold it firmly. Make sure your pelvis is pushed forwards and your torso is not sinking down. Knees, hips and shoulders must be in line. Keep the tension in this position.

Back exercises

Hoop lift from prone position

1. Take the starting position as shown in the illustration. Make sure your head and arms are slightly raised off the floor. Place your Hula Hoop on your forearms.

2. Now lift the Hula Hoop upwards with your arms. While doing this, pull your shoulder blades together. Imagine squeezing the Hula Hoop together. Always look down so that you do not overstretch your head. Lower the Hula Hoop slowly and in a controlled manner and return to the starting position.

Lat press

1. Take the starting position as shown in the illustration.

2. Now press your elbows into the floor with force and hold the hoop firmly so that your upper body is lifted. Then slowly lower again and do it again. Make sure that the force comes from the back muscles and not from the abdominal muscles (do not do a sit-up).

Back pull

1. Take the starting position as shown in the illustration.

2. Pull your Hula Hoop towards you. As you do this, pull your shoulder blades together and push your chest slightly forward. Make sure that your head does not move.

Diver

1. Take the starting position as shown in the illustration. Make sure your grip is more than shoulder width apart. The head is slightly raised so that your face does not touch the floor.

2. Pull the Hula Hoop behind your head by tensing the upper back muscles. During the exercise you can also slightly lift your legs to work the lower back muscles at the same time. Do not stretch your back upwards too much. Slowly return to the starting position.

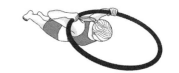

Arm, chest and shoulder exercises

One-arm triceps press

1. Take the starting position as shown in the illustration. Make sure the elbow of the arm holding the hoop is pointing straight up and is perpendicular to the floor.

2. Push the hoop upwards as shown in the illustration. As you do this, your elbow should move as little as possible. Extend your arm completely and hold the position for one second. Then return the arm to the starting position in a controlled manner.

Triceps press

1. Take the starting position as shown in the illustration.

2. Press the hoop upwards. Elbows should point forwards and move as little as possible. Fully extend the arms. Return to the starting position slowly and in a controlled manner.

Triceps kick backs

1. Take the starting position as shown in the illustration.

2. Push your hoop back and up by extending your arm. The upper arm should move as little as possible and remain parallel to the floor.

Knee push-up

1. Take the starting position as shown in the illustration.

2. Do a push-up. Hands should be about shoulder width apart and facing forwards. Shoulder blades should be pulled down and back during the exercise. Lower your body so that your nose touches the Hula Hoop. Keep your head straight. Then push yourself back up to the starting position.

Push-up

1. Take the starting position as shown in the illustration.

2. Do a push-up. Hands should be about shoulder width apart and facing forwards. Shoulder blades should be pulled down and back during the exercise. Lower your body so that your nose touches the Hula Hoop. Keep your head straight. Then push yourself back up to the starting position.

Front raises

1. Take the starting position as shown in the illustration.

2. Lift your hoop upwards with arms outstretched. Only the arms should move, shoulders remain pulled down. Make sure you don't hyperextend your back and keep your head straight.

3. Return to the starting position in a controlled manner.

Hoop Steering Wheel

1. Take the starting position as shown in the illustration. Make sure both arms are slightly bent.

2. Use your Hula Hoop like a steering wheel. Rotate your Hula Hoop back and forth as far as possible without letting go.

Shoulder press

1. Take the starting position as shown in the illustration.

2. Press your Hula Hoop over your head until your arms are fully extended.

3. Slowly return to the starting position.

Arm, chest and shoulder exercises | 138

Falling Hoop

1. Take the starting position as shown in the illustration.

2. Release the hoop with the top hand and lift the hoop upward with the other hand. This will cause the hoop to roll forwards.

3. Now grab the hoop at the bottom with your free hand and release it again with your other hand. Then lift the hoop up again with one hand and repeat.

Full Body Exercises

Front lift with back kick

1. Take the starting position as shown in the illustration.

2. Lift your hoop upward with your arms extended. During the upward movement, lift one leg as far back as possible. As you do this, your upper body will bend forward slightly. Make sure you keep the tension in your torso and do not hyperextend your back.
Return to the starting position in a controlled manner. Repeat the exercise with the same leg until the number of repetitions is reached. Then perform with the other leg.

Lateral leg raises

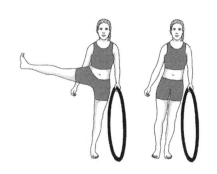

1. Take the starting position as shown in the illustration.

2. Lift one leg to the side. Use the Hula Hoop as a support.

3. Return the leg to the starting position in a controlled manner and repeat the exercise until the number of repetitions is reached. Then start with the other leg.

Hooping jack

1. Take the starting position as shown in the illustration.

2. Jump into a close stance and at the same time pull the Hula Hoop upwards with your arms.

3. Jump back to the starting position and lower the hoop down at the same time.

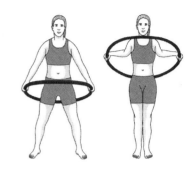

Hoop Steering Wheel Squat

1. Take the starting position as shown in the illustration. The deeper you get into the squat, the harder it gets. Make sure your knees stay above the center of your feet at all times.

2. Use your Hula Hoop like a steering wheel. Rotate your Hula Hoop back and forth as much as possible without letting go.

Squat with shoulder press

1. Take the starting position as shown in the illustration.

2. Squat. Make sure your knees do not reach over the top of your toes. Lower the hoop on the downward movement. Raise the hoop above your head on the upward movement.

Full Body Exercises | 140

Squat with hoop lift

1. Take the starting position as shown in the illustration.

2. Perform a supported squat. As you go up, simultaneously raise your extended arms above your head.

Hoop Burpees

1. Take a push-up position as shown in the illustration.

2. Perform a push-up. As you push up, keep your hands on the floor and jump into your Hula Hoop with your legs.

3. Now grab the hoop with your arms and straighten up as if you were doing a squat. As you do so, extend your arms with the hoop up over your head.

141 | Full Body Exercises

DISCLAIMER

This book contains opinions and ideas of the author and is intended to provide helpful and informative knowledge to people. The strategies contained may not suit every reader, and there is no guarantee that they will work for everyone. Use of this book and implementation of the information contained therein is expressly at your own risk. Liability claims against the author for damages of a material or non-material nature caused by the use or non-use of the information or by the use of incorrect and/or incomplete information are expressly excluded. The work, including all content, does not guarantee or warrant the timeliness, accuracy, completeness or quality of the information provided. Misprints and misinformation can not be completely excluded.

Imprint

pisionary Verlag (pisionary publishing)
Author is represented by: Dominik Ilse
Geppinger Straße 28, 83404 Ainring (Germany)
Year of publication: 2021